Tales of a
Magic Monastery

Tales of a
Magic Monastery

Theophane the Monk

Crossroad · New York

1987

The Crossroad Publishing Company
370 Lexington Avenue, New York, N.Y. 10017

Printed in the United States of America

Library of Congress
Cataloging in Publication Data

Theophane the Monk.
Tales of a Magic Monastery.

1. Spiritual life—Catholic authors. I. Title.
BX2350.2.T486   248.4   81-9765
ISBN 0-8245-0085-7   AACR2

Contents

all these stories are true

I

re You Rich or Are You Poor?

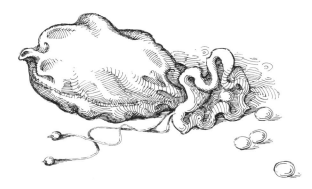

The Pearl of Great Price

He asked me what I was looking for.

"Frankly," I said, "I'm looking for the Pearl of Great Price."

He slipped his hand into his pocket, drew it out, AND GAVE IT TO ME. It was just like that! I was dumbfounded. Then I began to protest: "You don't want to give it to *me*? Don't you want to keep it for yourself? But . . ."

When I kept this up, he said finally, "Look, is it better to *have* the Pearl of Great Price, or to give it away?"—

Well, now I have it. I don't tell anyone. From some there would just be disbelief and ridicule. "You, you have the Pearl of Great Price? Hah!" Others would be jealous, or someone might steal it. Yes, I *do* have it. But there's that question—"Is it better to have it, or to give it away?" How long will that question rob me of my joy?

A Visit from the Buddha

Why did I visit the Magic Monastery? Well, I'm a monk myself, and the strangest thing happened in my monastery. We had a visit from the Buddha. We prepared for it, and gave him a very warm, though solemn, welcome. He stayed overnight, but he slipped away very early in the morning. When the monks woke up, they found graffiti all over the cloister walls. Imagine! And do you know what he wrote? One word—TRIVIA—TRIVIA—TRIVIA—all over the place.

Well, we were in a rage. But then when I quieted down I looked about and realized, "Yes, it is true." So much of what I saw was trivia, and most of what I heard. But what is worse, when I closed my eyes, all inside was trivia. For several weeks this was my experience, and my very efforts to rectify it just made it worse. I left my monastery and headed for the Magic Monastery.

The Brother showed me around. First, the Hall of Laughter. Everything fed the flame of laughter, big things and small, sacred, solemn, inconsequential. Only laughter there.

Next, the Room of Sorrow. The very essence of bitter tears—those of the bereaved mother, the lonely, depressed. *Only* sorrow here.

Now the Hall of Words. Words upon words, spoken and written. Alone they must have had some sense, but all together—total confusion. I cried out, "Stop! Stop!" but I was only adding words to words.

Next, the great Hall of Silence. Here there is no time.

He took me finally to the Hall of Treasures. "Take anything you want," he whispered.

I chose the heart of Jesus, and with it I am heading back to my monastery.

The Great Debate

I had been a few years in another monastery and things were not going well. I persuaded someone to inquire around and find out what the other monks thought of me. His report—"They call you Nobody."

That was terrible to hear. Some of the people in my head started shouting in a rage, "No I'm SOMEBODY, somebody." Others moaned, "No, it's true; you are Nobody." The great debate. It went on for months, all in my head. It wore me out. "Somebody!" "Nobody!" "Somebody!" "Nobody!"

Once night someone came into my room, got on his knees, and put his forehead to the ground. I thought he was mocking me, so I just ignored him. After a while I gained courage and began to curse at him. When finally I spat at him, he spoke. "Please come to the

Magic Monastery." I tried to make some reply, but the words came out all stutters and stammers. That debate was tearing me apart. He just put out his hand. I took it and followed him.

As we walked up the path to the great door, the bells began to ring—as if there were a great feast. The Abbot came to greet me and led me into a huge hall. He placed me in the center, and the monks and nuns, hundreds of them, came and sat all around me. Someone brought the candle from the sanctuary to set in front of me. And so we sat, all through the night. Now you might say they sat in silence, their eyes closed. But this is the Magic Monastery, and my experience was different. I heard them chanting "Somebody, Somebody . . . at last, at last . . . Welcome, welcome." I heard the Abbot tell them how I had just got in from Egypt. We were all breathing as one. Someone invited me to sing for them. I said I couldn't sing, but I'd tell them a few jokes. One said it was good to have a new perspective. Then someone called out, "You can sing." So I sang; I sang the song of my life—my past, my present, my future. It was so beautiful.

II

How Big Is Your Heart?

Myself?

I sat there in awe as the old monk answered our questions. Though I'm usually shy, I felt so comfortable in his presence that I found myself raising my hand. "Father, could you tell us something about yourself?"

He leaned back. "Myself?" he mused. There was a long pause.

"My name . . .
   used to be . . .
   Me.

But now . . .
   it's you."

The Best Place To Pray

I asked an old monk, "How do I get over the habit of judging people?"

He answered, "When I was your age, I was wondering where would be the best place to go to pray. Well, I asked Jesus that question. His answer was, 'Why don't you go into the heart of my Father?' So I did. I went into the heart of the Father, and all these years that's where I've prayed. Now I see everyone as my own child. How can I judge anyone?"

The House of Perfect Love

As I was strolling around the grounds, I came across one building with a sign outside: "House of Perfect Love." Don't ask me why I didn't go in. I didn't even look in, but hurried away.

The next morning, when I was leaving, I saw a beggar at the foot of the hill, and stopped to give him some money. "Why are you weeping?" he asked.

"Me? I'm not weeping."

"You're not weeping outside, but you're weeping inside."

It was true. I was weeping inside because I hadn't been man enough to go into that house. I was afraid there'd be a cross there.

When I admitted this to him, he said, "I can understand that. My own name used to be Fear. I know that sometimes we just *can't* go into the *magic* place—but then maybe we can go into the REAL place. And sometimes it's the other way around—we can manage the magic place, but not yet the REAL place. Why don't you sit down here beside me? Together we'll go into the real House of Perfect Love. People won't suspect a thing. They'll just think we're poor beggars. They'll look down on us, and give us their money."

God bless that beggar.

What Am I Leaving Out?

I knew there were many interesting sights, but I didn't want any more of the LITTLE answers. I wanted the big answer. So I asked the guestmaster to show me to the House of the Christian God.

I sat myself down, quite willing to wait for the big answer. I remained silent all day, far into the night. I looked Him in the eye. I guess He was looking me in the eye. Late, late at night I seemed to hear a voice, "What are you leaving out?" I looked around. I heard it again, "What are you leaving out?" Was it my imagination? Soon it was all around me, whispering, roaring, "What are you leaving out? WHAT ARE YOU LEAVING OUT?"

Was I cracking up? I managed to get to my feet and head for the door. I guess I wanted the comfort of a human face or a human

voice. Nearby was the corridor where some of the monks live. I knocked on one cell.

"What do you want?" came a sleepy voice.

"What am I leaving out?"

"Me," he answered.

I went to the next door.

"What do you want?"

"What am I leaving out?"

"Me."

A third cell, a fourth, all the same.

I thought to myself, "They're all stuck on themselves." I left the building in disgust. Just then the sun was coming up. I had never spoken to the sun before, but I heard myself pleading, "What am I leaving out?"

The sun too answered, "Me." That finished me.

I threw myself flat on the ground. Then the earth said, "ME."

III

s This What It Means
To Be A Real Monk?

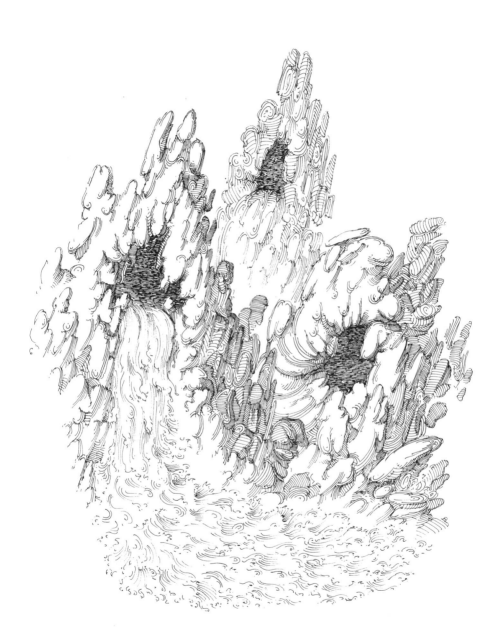

The Monk Whose Face Was Red

Standing beside a cave was a monk whose face was red, I mean really red. He smiled at me and said, "I guess you're wondering why my face is so red."

I sure was. "Well, it was this way. When I was fifty I died. When I went to judgment, they asked me, 'What have you accomplished?' That's when my face turned red. I pleaded with them to give me more time. 'All right,' they said, 'we'll give you seven more years.'

"So I came back to my cave. I went in and kept going. I went in deeper than I'd ever gone before, in and down, in and down. I must have walked for several days, although it was so dark I couldn't tell day from night. I just wanted to get away from people; my face was so red. And I wanted time to think, to think about how I would spend those seven years. But it was scary. I didn't know what I'd meet down there, and I wasn't sure I'd be able to find my way back. I kept going.

"Finally I began to hear a rumbling sound, like mighty waters. You know what it was? It was the tears of the whole world! I heard the bitter tears of EVERYONE'S fear, hurt, despair, disappointment, rage. Everyone's. And I heard the sweet tears too—you know, when you're loved, when you're safe at last, a loved one restored, those tears of joy. Yes, I heard the death of Christ and his resurrection. I must have been at the heart of the earth, because, while I couldn't hear any words, I heard ALL the tears and therefore I experienced total communion. I was separated from my separateness.

I don't know how long I stayed there in that state of total communion—days, weeks. But I finally decided how I would spend my seven years. I would go back to the mouth of the cave and conduct people back and forth to the depths.

A Creature of Contraction and Expansion

I am a monk myself, and the one question I really wanted to ask was, "What is a monk?" Well, I finally did, but for an answer I got a most peculiar question: "Do you mean in the daytime or at night?" Now what could that mean?

When I didn't answer, he picked it up again, "A monk, like everyone else, is a creature of contraction and expansion. During the day he is contracted—behind his cloister walls, dressed in a habit like all the others, doing the routine things you expect a monk to do. At night he expands. The walls cannot contain him. He moves throughout the world and he touches the stars.

"Ah," I thought, "poetry." To bring him down to earth I began to ask, "Well, during the day, in his REAL body . . ."

"Wait," he said, "that's the difference between us and you. You people regularly assume that the contracted state is the real body. It IS real, in a sense. But here we tend to start from the other end, the expanded state. The daytime state we refer to as the 'body of fear.' And whereas you tend to judge a monk by his decorum during the day, we tend to measure a monk by the number of persons he touches at night, and the number of stars."

The Crystal Globe

I told the guestmaster I'd like to become a monk.

"What kind of monk?" he asked. "A real monk?"

"Yes," I said.

He poured me a cup of wine. "Here, take this." No sooner had I drunk it than I became aware of a crystal globe forming around me. It began to expand until finally it surrounded him too. This monk, who a minute before had seemed so commonplace, now took on an astonishing beauty. I was struck dumb. After a bit the thought came to me, "Maybe I should tell him how beautiful he is—perhaps he doesn't even know."

But I really *was* dumb—that wine had burned out my tongue! But so great was my happiness at the sight of such beauty that I thought it was well worth the price of my tongue. When he made me a sign to leave, I turned away, confident that the memory of that beauty would be a joy forever.

But what was my surprise when I found that with each person I met it was the same—as soon as he would pass unwittingly into my crystal globe, I could see his beauty too. And I knew it was real.

Is this what it means to be a REAL monk—to see the beauty in others and to be silent?

IV

here Is the Answer to the Great Question?

The Original Sound

I asked an old monk, "How long have you been here?"

"Forever," he answered.

"I smiled. "Fifty years, Father?"

"Forever."

Did you know St. Benedict?"

"We are novices together."

"Did you know Jesus?"

"He and I converse every day."

I threw away my silly smile, fell to my knees, and clutched his hand. "Father," I whispered, "Did you hear the original sound?"

"I am listening to the original sound."

It's Very Simple

He looked so holy that I simply asked him, "Tell me what God is like."

With feather gentleness he replied, "It is Lent now. I'm accustomed to refrain from talking during Lent. But take this book." (It was the book he had been writing in.) "If you read this at the right hour, it will tell you what God is like."

I couldn't wait to bring it back and share it with my wife.

Back home, she was a little less excited than I about the book, because her mind was on our first child that she was carrying. "What did he mean by 'at the right hour?'" she asked.

I didn't know. We began to speculate. Maybe at noon on Good Friday. Maybe after the Easter Vigil. Maybe at the moment when we are in deep distress. Perhaps we should wait for God to reveal to

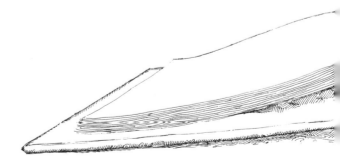

us the right hour. It might even be years from now. We decided we'd better wait for a sign.

Two weeks later my first son was born. How can I tell you what it was like? First the worry, then—that child. I was a father. You grow up when you become a father. When I looked at that child I was so proud. I knew I was somebody. And yet humbled. I scarcely knew how to hold him, much less to bring him up. I used to think I had it all figured out, but that kid was bigger than I.

That night the child appeared to me in a dream. "What is God like?" he asked.

That did it. I got up and reached for the book. I brought it to my wife and told her, "This is the right hour. We'll open it now."

I opened it at random. I read, "It's very simple. God is a father."

My wife opened it again. She read, "It's very simple. God became a little child."

"Let's open it again." I cried, "together." I took her hand. She opened it, and we read, "It's very simple. Each breath you breathe is the breath of God."

Infinite Respect

Did you ever hear a sermon begin with the words, "When I was in heaven"? That's how the old monk began his rap with us, "When I was in heaven . . ."

"When I was in heaven, they gave me a torch with which I could see EVERYTHING.

"Everything—do you believe me? Of course I couldn't see *myself,* but I really could see everything else. Oh, I reveled in it—the beauty, the connections, the great dance. I was dancing the great dance! That went on for several years, but then came a time when seeing everything became an embarrassment. I had trouble fitting what I saw into their words. And they had trouble fitting me into their schools. So increasingly I would set aside the torch and rely on their flashlights and fluorescents and books. One day I hid the torch under a bushel somewhere and proceeded to forget all about it. I just went forward with their flashlights and fluorescents and books.

"And that's the way I lived, many years. I became what they call a theologian. I, the Teacher, led the way! But once I brought a group of college students here on retreat. They were rather like you. They were fascinated with the place and with the monk who was talking with them.

"Then one of them asked the question that changed my life. He asked, 'Do you believe in guardian angels?' I was embarrassed. How would the poor monk answer that one?

"But no difficulty for him. 'No, I don't *believe* in guardian angels. A guardian angel is one who gazes on the glory of God, and at the same time specializes in your welfare. He is the messenger between God and you. That is what the word "angel" means. Why don't you close your eyes? Now ask your guardian angel for a message from God.'

"We did, and I did, and the message I got was 'Infinite Respect.' 'Infinite Respect'—the whole world changed. I can no longer bear to be called a theologian, or a teacher. I do what I can. I serve, I share. My angel has told me about heaven, and about the torch I used to have. Someday it will be mine again, but meanwhile, though I realize I am blind, whenever anyone comes into this room, my angel whispers 'Infinite Respect,' and my spirit prostrates before God in that person."

Surrounded by God

As soon as I passed through the gate of the monastery I felt surrounded—surrounded by God. It wasn't as if He was in heaven, or in church, or even in my heart. He was all around me.

That's the way it was—all day long. And then all night long, and the next day. I didn't have to *do* anything. God was just there.

I had come expecting to spend a lot of time praying and reading, but I found myself just chatting with people, and scrubbing floors, and strolling around. God was always there.

On the sixth day a little kid *fixed* it—for good. "Hi, Sonny," I said to him. "I'm so happy here, I feel like a kid myself."

His reply was, "I know how it is. Why don't you try to escape?"

V

ould You Go Deeper?

What Do They Need?

There's a monk there who will never give you advice, but only a question. I was told his questions could be very helpful. I sought him out. "I am a parish priest," I said. "I'm here on retreat. Could you give me a question?"

"Ah, yes," he answered. "My question is, 'What do they need?'"

I came away disappointed. I spent a few hours with the question, writing out answers, but finally I went back to him.

"Excuse me. Perhaps I didn't make myself clear. Your question has been helpful, but I wasn't so much interested in thinking about my apostolate during this retreat. Rather I wanted to think seriously about my own spiritual life. Could you give me a question for my own spiritual life?"

"Ah, I see. Then my question is, 'What do they REALLY need?'"

Write My Own Bible?

I've been going there on retreat each year for the past forty years. Each time it's the same, yet somehow always different. The first time I went I forgot to bring my Bible. When I asked the guestmaster if I could borrow a Bible, he said. "Wouldn't you care to write your own?" "What do you mean?" "Well, write your own Bible—something of your own on the order of the Bible. You could tell of a classical bondage and the great liberation, a promised land, sacred songs, a messiah—that kind of thing. Ought to be much more interesting than just reading someone else's Bible. And you might learn more."

Well, I set to work. It took me a month. I never learned so much about the official Bible. When I was finished, he recommended I take it home and try to live according to it for a year. I should keep a journal of my experience. But I shouldn't tell anybody about the project, nor show anyone the books. Next year, after Christmas I could come back for another retreat.

It was quite a year. An eyeopener. Most certainly I had never put so much energy and alertness into living by the official Bible as I was putting into living by this one. And my daily meditations had never been so concentrated.

When I arrived back for my next retreat, he greeted me very warmly, took into his hands my Bible and my journal, kissed them with greatest reverence, and told me I could now spend a couple days and nights in the Hall of the Great Fire. On the last night of the year, I should consign my two books to the flames. And that's what I did. A whole year's wisdom and labor—into the Great Fire. Afterwards he set me to work writing another Bible.

And so it went, these past forty years. Each year a new Bible, a new journal, and then at the end of the year—into the flames. Until now I have never told anyone about this.

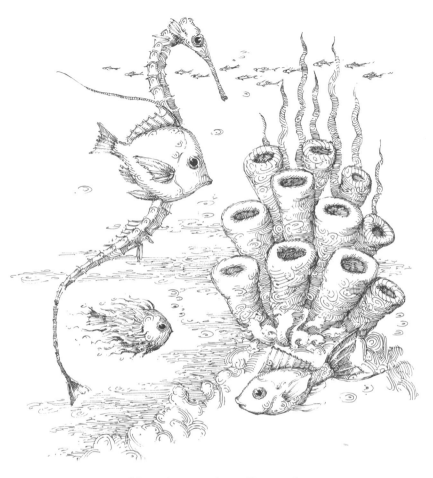

Back to the Depths

When I was a kid I lived near the Magic Monastery. I used to go there every Saturday. Mostly I'd swim in their lake. Marvelous lake, once into it, you would find it had the dimensions of an ocean. I'd swim down and down. It took me a couple hours to get to the bottom. Down there were three mermaids I got to know. We'd have a lot of fun. We'd dance around. Dancing is different in the water.

And we'd hunt for sunken treasure—and find it. With a bow we would give each other gifts—some precious gems, or a piece of coral, or driftwood, or something someone else had thrown away. Any gift was far more precious than money. And we could always find something to laugh about together. By nightfall I had to be back. Sundays there was Church. Monday to Friday school. I guess I lived for my Saturdays. It had its effect on me. Some people thought I was pretty deep. Others thought I was all wet. Some wondered if I would ever grow up.

Then came the day when one of the monks told me I was getting too old to swim in the lake. I couldn't understand that at all. What did age have to do with it? Well, I thought, why go to the Magic Monastery at all if they won't let me swim in the lake. So I stayed away. I stayed away many years.

But yesterday I went back. It was this way: You see, I became a writer, and a respected lecturer. Yesterday I gave THE lecture of my career. It went over very well. It will be written up in all the papers. People said it was really profound. But when I was home alone, sitting in my recliner, the thought came to me, "Am I so deep after all?" Right then and there I returned to my Magic Monastery, ran down into the water, and swam down, down, down. At last at the bottom there were my old friends. The mermaids were thrilled to see me again, and I them. They wanted to know all about what I had been doing. I told them about my successful career writing and my lecturing. When they pressed me for more information, I said, "Fortunately I have my briefcase here." (Actually I always carry it with me, even swimming.) "You can read for yourself some of my better lectures, including one I gave this very day, before a very important audience."

One of them took it and began to read aloud. Would you believe it—the others began to laugh. Seeing my embarrassment, they apologized, but they were soon convulsed with laughter. Well, in the depth of an ocean, I want you to know, laughter really travels. Soon all sorts of sea creatures were picking up the vibrations and coming closer to share the fun. At last I myself had to join in the laughter. As the mermaid went on reading my masterpiece, the ocean was like one giant washing machine, all awash with laughter. Besides the mermaids and me there were bluefish and greyfish, dolphins and sharks, whales and octopi, minnows and sponges—you name it.

When at last, exhausted, we all fell quiet, you should have heard the silence. There's no silence like that of the ocean deep. It would have been dreadful to be alone there.

VI

*hen?*

Now

I had just one desire—to give myself completely to God. So I headed for the monastery. An old monk asked me, "What is it you want?"

I said, "I just want to give myself to God."

I expected him to be gentle, fatherly, but he *shouted* at me, "NOW!" I was stunned. He shouted again, "NOW!" Then he reached for a club and came after me. I turned and ran. He kept coming aftr me, brandishing his club and shouting, "Now, Now."

That was years ago. He still follows me, wherever I go. Always that stick, always that "NOW!"

Next Monday?

I had heard that there was a monk there who had been to Tabor—present at the Transfiguration—imagine! I found him. You couldn't miss him—that face would stand out anywhere.

"Father," I said, "what was it like?"

"Well, we went up the mountain, and Jesus began to pray. Other people only partly pray. He prayed *totally*. My companions were taken by the light, but it was the *sound* that got to me. It was music, but you never heard music like that. It just took over my whole body and soul. Then, when the cloud came, he passed into it, and I did too. That's all I can say. I've been pretty useless ever since. I just live here with Him, in that music, in that cloud."

"Father," I whispered, "call me in."

"Do you want to come in now, " he asked, "or next Monday?"

"O Father, call me in now. I've waited long enough."

He took my head to his heart, and I heard that music. The cloud settled around us.

VII

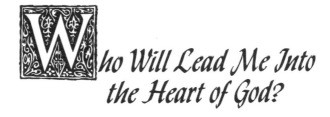

ho Will Lead Me Into
the Heart of God?

Together

I thought it good fortune to go to the Magic Monastery for Christmas. But at the foot of the hill sat a blind beggar, and when I drew near to give him some money, I heard him ask, "Who will lead me into the heart of God?"

I couldn't go on. Who would lead him into the heart of God?

I sat down in front of him. I took his hands. "Together," I said. "Together we'll go into the heart of God."

The Great Silence

"Would you teach me silence?" I asked.

"Ah!"

He seemed to be pleased. "Is it the Great Silence that you want?"

"Yes, the Great Silence."

"Well, where do you think it's to be found?" he asked.

"Deep within me, I suppose. If only I could go deep within, I'm sure I'd escape the noise at last. But it's hard. Will you help me?" I knew he would. I could feel his concern, and his spirit was so silent.

"Well, I've been there," he answered. "I spent years going in. I did taste the silence there. But one day Jesus came—maybe it was my imagination—and said to me simply, 'Come, follow me.' I went out, and I've never gone back."

I was stunned. "But the silence . . ."

"I've found the Great Silence, and I've come to see that the noise was inside."

So Small Outside

I came there looking for my brother. They told me, "Try that little building over there." Well, I had tried every place else, so I went.

Strangest thing—so small outside, it was vast inside, and sure enough, I found my brother there.

David's Flute

I went there as a child. There was an old monk sitting under a tree playing a flute. I was fascinated. When he stopped playing, I said, "That sounds like Christmas. Could you tell me a Christmas story?"

"Aha!"—he laughed. "Christmas? I was there. I was there, my boy. Sit down. Sit down. The others are tired of hearing my story.

"You see, it was like this: I had two flutes in those days. One I would play during the day, the other at night. The one I played during the day was your ordinary type of flute. The one I played at night was special. It could not be heard by human ears—that way the other shepherds could get their sleep. But ah, the angels could hear it. Yes, the angels heard it, and they would come whenever I played. They would turn out in great numbers. I had quite a few friends among the angels, my boy. Do you have a few angel friends?

"Well look, one night when I finished playing, all the angels slipped away—except one. He came close. There was a secret in his eyes. He bent over and whispered into my ear. The Big Secret! My boy, the Big Secret!

"The next evening I persuaded the other shepherds to come with me. I just told them a child had been born. Everyone loves a child. When we got there, they went right in to admire the child and congratulate the parents. But I—I just fell flat on my face. What else could I do? Finally the father pulled me to my feet. 'I see you have two flutes,' he said. 'Would you play for the child?'

"'Ah, no,' I answered, 'neither of these will do. This one is just for humans, and this one is just for angels.'

"The father laughed. 'I see,' he said. 'Well, I am a carpenter, and my father was too. But one of our ancestors was, like you, a shepherd. He used to play the flute. But then, after they made him king, why he felt he really shouldn't play that flute anymore. He just stored it away. They found it when he died. It has been handed down from father to son, these many generations. They say it's for the good shepherd. I've never let anyone play it, but tonight I'm so happy. Here—take it. Play it—please.'

"I played. My boy, the angels sure heard it that night. And the stars too. That was my great hour. I called out *all* the angels, and all the stars."

"Well, that carpenter let me keep the flute. This is it. I'm getting old now. I'd like to pass it on. But who wants it? They all prefer words! Imagine—they think they can announce the Big Secret with words!"

VIII

ho Needs Me?

Beautiful, Worthwhile, Noble

When I was young I went to the Magic Monastery, hoping to join. I expected to be questioned and asked to get letters of recommendation. Instead, the monk handed me a book. "Here, take this. It's a blank book. Each day you can write down on one page what you have done that day that's beautiful, worthwhile, noble. When you've filled the book that way, you can come back. We'll look through it and see if we want to take you. And here—here's a pencil for you—with an eraser."

Well, I went home and set to work. Each day I tried to think of something beautiful, worthwhile, noble, to do. And at the end of the day I'd write it down, with some satisfaction. But regularly, a few days later, or a few weeks later, when I'd reread it, it would seem so paltry. Then I'd use my eraser.

Well, that was more than thirty years ago. I've long since used up the pencil and worn down the eraser. And I gave the book away. How can I go to the Magic Monastery? They need me here. And I need them.

The Well

Up there each one gets what he wants. I came there a wounded man, sorely hurt by my brothers. I went to the well as directed and shouted down: "Solitude!" And that's what I got. What a relief! You have no idea. How I needed that rest.

After a few years, however, I began to long for community. I thought of the example and teaching of Christ. Was it right to be alone so much? So I went to the well. "Community," I shouted. I got it. Beautiful—for a while.

Well, there were ups and downs. At one point it got so distressing that I went to the well and shouted, "Death." I died. Peace at last. My troubles were over. I really enjoyed it.

It wasn't long, though, before I got to thinking, "Well, life—at least you're alive—it isn't all that bad. It's up to you. It's what you make of it. And you can help people. Here—what can I do?"

I began to wish I could go to the well and get back my life. But I couldn't get there, and if I could have, I had no breath to shout. I was just dead. Couldn't someone else go and shout for me? It didn't seem to occur to them. They saw me lying there, but no one thought to bring me back to life. Why were they so thoughtless, so selfish?

At last someone did think of it. He went to the well and called down, "Life for my brother." I rose from the dead. Oh, to be alive again, to breathe, to see, to walk, to hear, to relate to people.

But where was that man who raised me up? I asked everyone I met, "Have you seen the man who raised me from the dead?" They thought I was crazy. "No one comes back from the grave." "Called down the well for you? You call down for yourself, not for someone else." I searched all over. And you know, I passed many a grave before it finally occurred to me that someone else might be longing to return to life. I ran to the well. "Life for my brothers!" Ah, then I saw in the water way down there the face of the one who raised me from the dead.

IX

What Is Your Gift?

The Audacity of Humility

I walked up to an old, old monk and asked him, "What is the audacity of humility?" This man had never met me before, but do you know what his answer was? "To be the first to say 'I love you.'"

The Woman Who Wanted Greatness

She is tiny. When she first went there, she was asked, "What is it you want?"

She answered, "I'm very short, and I'm a woman. I feel many doors closed to me. What is it I want? I want GREATNESS. I want greatness before I die."

Impressed, the monk said to her, "There is a man on a cross." He took her hand and led her to Calvary. She ran up without dignity, threw herself at his feet and just kissed them, kissed them. There she stayed, for three hours, her tears running down the hill.

And now, when you go to the Magic Monastery, and you don't have the guts to go to Calvary, she'll come out and wash your feet with her tears. Then she dries them with her hair. You become great. I *know* this. I can't tell you how small I was before she kissed my feet.

What Do I Need To Know?

People were sitting around asking him questions. His answers were so beautiful. When the others had run out of questions, there was a long silence. Then I heard myself asking, "What do I need to know?"

He didn't answer. Just kept looking at me—for several minutes. Tears began to run down his cheek. But he looked happy enough.

Someone nudged me. "Ask him another question."

"No," he said. "That's the best question. I was thinking of the time I asked that very question of my master—when I first entered the monastery, fifty years ago. I will tell you how my master answered. He told me to take that question, 'what do I need to know?' and put it to every single monk. I did. Then he had me sit in solitude for a year, reflecting on their answers. Next he had me find a ship and sail around the world, putting my question to everyone I met. That took me six years. And I had to reflect on the answers in solitude for six years. That's how my master answered my question."

The room became silent again. "But Sir," I insisted, "please, what do *I* need to know?"

"Good," he answered. "I will give you—Christ, and that will be enough."

You'll Find It Very Handy

When the guestmaster asked me what my spiritual practice was, I told him, "The Rosary. I've been saying that every day for years. I have a great devotion to Our Lady."

"Would you like to meet her?" he asked.

"What do you mean?"

"Well, she's right over there, the door at the end of the cloister."

"You mean I could have an appointment?"

"No appointment, just go in." I did. There she was, no mistaking it. She remained in her chair, but her eyes and face embraced me as if I were her infant. Then she spoke my name. That surprised me. Why did that surprise me, when I had been praying to her for so many years? I was speechless. She took my head to her heart.

Then after a bit she began to speak. It was reminiscing. She went back to my infancy, told me about my parents, my childhood, adolescence, then went right up to the present. But she saw it all so differently. It was a total reinterpretation of my life. Finally, she said, "Before you go, I want to give you something. It's my Amen. You'll find it very handy. You can use it in all sorts of situations. You can apply it to persons and memories. It will grow with use, and hopefully some day you will say the Great Amen."

I live now in the embrace of those eyes. Daily I use her Amen. Please pray for me that some day I may dare to say the Great Amen.

X

What Color Is Your Robe?

The Monk in the Red Robe

There's a monk there who wears a red robe. I was wondering why, but it was my little son who dared to ask him why. "Mister, why are you wearing that red dress?"

"Sit down, sonny, and I'll tell you. When I was your age I used to dream about becoming a monk. I knew that monks usually wore white robes, but in my dreams I was usually wearing green. When I got older I got my parents' blessing and went off to become a monk. But I went searching all around for a monastery where the monks wore green. No one had ever heard of such a place, but I thought surely there was some place that corresponded to my dream.

"Ah, the beautiful monasteries I saw! The holiness! I saw monks who lived on a very high mountain. God spoke to them face to face. They never came down from their mountaintop monastery but would extend their hands in blessing over all the peoples of the earth.

"There was a monastery in the jungle. Every evening when the monks sang vespers the wild animals would come around in a great

circle and sway with the rhythm. Lions, tigers, crocodiles—I saw them with my own eyes.

"I would tell you more, but your father will be weary. For many years I traveled from monastery to monastery. I would stay a few months, a few years, but always I moved on—in search of the monastery of my dreams. After many years I met an old sailor who knew of a monastery where the monks wore green. It was on a small island in the middle of the ocean, he said. The monks seemed all to be children. They would play and sing and laugh all day long. And they wore green—he was sure they wore green. He offered to take me there. But a great fear came over me. To become a child again? Do I really want that? I told him I'd need some time to think about it. Did I really want that? Two weeks later he sailed off without me.

"By this time, since I had spent so many years living in many monasteries, people thought of me as a monk, and I guess I thought of myself as a monk. But when that sailor sailed off without me, I knew what I was made of. I settled down here and asked the abbot to give me a red robe. It distinguishes me from the real monks, and it catches the eye of children."

The Room of Righteous Indignation

The guestmaster looked at me carefully and lead me to a room marked "Righteous Indignation."

"Good," I thought, "back home some people don't understand me. They think I'm judgmental. But this man understands."

There wasn't much in the room besides the four walls, and that was all right with me. I sat down and meditated a while. Then I read my Bible. I found myself looking at those walls. I read some more, then meditated, then looked at the walls again. Late in the evening, as I was staring at one of the walls, it became transparent, and I found myself looking at my own monastery. Fascinating. What's more, as I watched, I found I could see right through its walls and into its church and cloisters.

After a while I could even see inside the cell of each monk. I saw everything. I saw what each monk had in his room and what he was doing. I saw some praying, some sleeping, some reading. I could even see what each one was reading. Brother! Do you see what that one is reading? And look at the private property! Soon I could hear their voices. I could hear everything that was said—the complaints, the backbiting. My own name was mentioned. Huh—that one to be complaining of me!

I began to take notes. I filled page after page. I had thought the place was bad before, but here were the facts—what they said, what they did, what they had. Nothing subjective—just cold facts. As I kept writing, I began to see right into their heads, to see their very thoughts. These also I wrote down.

Once, when I was resting my eyes, the thought came to me, "I wonder what I would see if the other wall were transparent?" Perhaps if I kept looking at it long enough. . . . Well, it did open up and through it I saw the Magic Monastery, every bit of it. What an eyeful! I thought my own place was bad. Talk about individualism. I began to write that down too.

I rang for the Brother and asked him to bring me some more notebooks. There was so much to get down. From time to time a further question would come to me, "I wonder what's behind these other two walls?" I became uncomfortable. "Who is there? What are the walls hiding? Why don't they let me see? It's probably dreadful." I took to staring at these walls. The Brother said that behind the one wall were the deceased members of the Magic Monastery, and behind the other were the deceased members of my own monastery.

"Ah," I said, "but why can't I see them? I want to see them."

"You won't like it," he said.

"Truth, that's all I want. That's all I've ever wanted. I call a spade a spade. Show me!"

"You'll only get angry."

"Show me. Bring me some more notebooks, and show me."

But he refused and hurried away. I was determined that when he returned the next day I would get the truth out of him.

I did. I took him by the throat and demanded to know what was going on behind those walls. "Behind this one," he gasped, "are the deceased members of your own community. They are all looking in at you. They are weeping and praying for you.

"Behind this other wall are all the deceased members of the Magic Monastery. They are all looking at you and laughing."

The Problem is Heaviness

Let me tell you something that happened on the last day of my retreat. I told the guestmaster that I didn't think I'd be able to get back soon because I wouldn't have the time. He came right back with "The problem is not TIME; the problem is HEAVINESS."

He turned and went downstairs, returning with a little carpet. "Here, take this. It is a magic carpet. If you'll just sit on it and let go of your heaviness, you can go anywhere you want. It's not a question of time."

I have come to know that this is true. People laugh at me when I tell them. Will you laugh too? All right. Then stay there.

XI

Still Holding Out?

What Will You Give Me?

Strange sight—a monk with no legs sat by the wall, calling out to passersby, "What will you give me? What will you give me?"

I felt compelled to stop and apologize: "I am a monk myself, so I have nothing to give you."

"Give me your unhappiness," he demanded. I did.

The Two Brothers

They told me the story of two monks who were blood brothers. The younger one had offended the older, and the older just could not forgive him. Every morning the younger one would knock on the door of his brother and call out, "Forgive me, Brother." But he would not. Day after day this went on, year after year.

After many years, the younger brother did not show up one morning. Nor the next, nor the next. The older one became uneasy. Finally he went out to look for his brother. He knocked on every door. "Have you seen my brother?" No one had. He left the monastery, knocked on the doors of all the neighbors. "Have you seen my brother?" He kept going. Miles away from the monastery he would knock on a door. "Have you seen my brother?" People thought him strange, but he kept it up. Days went by, months, years. And that was all he had to say, except that when someone would show annoyance he would say "Forgive me, Brother."

At last, after so many years of searching, he found himself back at his monastery. He knocked. The young Brother who answered did not recognize him, but was struck by the beauty of his face. He ran to call the others. They all came, crowding around. They were all struck by the beauty of this old man. Now some of the older ones recognized him. When they called out his name, he fell on his face. "Forgive me, Brothers," he said.

They wept, all of them.

Well, they made up a cell for him right beside the abbot's cell. And now, whenever any monk has difficulty forgiving his brother, why, he just slips in there for a few minutes. And guests can do the same.

The Mountain of Decision

"How long have you been a monk?" I asked.

"A real monk? Not long. It took me fifty years to get up the Mountain of Decision."

"Do you have to see first before you decide, or is it that you decide first and then you see?"

"If you'll take my advice," he said, "you'll drop the questions, and go right up the mountain."

Excuses

"Why not?" that was the first thing he said. He had never seen me before. I hadn't said a word. "Why not?" I knew he had me.

I brought up excuses: "My wife . . . the people I have to work with . . . not enough time . . . I guess it's my temperament . . ."

There was a sword hanging on the wall. He took it and gave it to me. "Here, with this sword, you can cut through any barriers." I took it and slipped away without saying a word.

Back in my room in the guesthouse I sat down and kept looking at that sword. I knew that what he said was true.

But the next day I returned his sword. How can I live without my excuses?

The Gun

I saw a monk working alone in the vegetable garden. I squatted down beside him and said, "Brother, what is your dream?"

It didn't seem to bother him that I should ask so personal a question, not even having the courtesy to introduce myself. He just looked straight at me (what a beautiful face he had) and answered, "I would like to become a monk."

"But Brother, you *are* a monk, aren't you?"

"I've been here twenty-five years, but I still carry my gun." He drew a revolver from a holster under his robe. It looked so strange, a monk holding a gun.

"And they won't let you become a monk until you give up your gun?"

"No, it's not that. Most of them don't even know I have it. But *I* know."

"Well, why *don't* you give it up?"

"I guess because I've had it so long. I've been hurt a lot, and I've hurt others. I don't think I could be comfortable without this gun."

"But you seem pretty uncomfortable *with* it."

"Yes, pretty uncomfortable. But I have my dream."

"Why don't you give me your gun," I whispered. I was beginning to tremble.

He did. He gave it to me. His tears ran down on the ground. He embraced me.

That was ten years ago. I still have that gun. Carry it with me all the time. I wouldn't feel comfortable without it.

Boredom

On my way up there I met a beggar and went over to give him some money. (My saintly mother had taught me never to pass a beggar without giving him something.) But he took my quarter and, with a look of disdain, flipped it into the bushes. "I don't need your money," he barked. "Why don't you give me your boredom?"

What could I say? I heard myself saying, "I'll have to ask my wife." And I hurried on before he could devastate me further.

Well, there were other things I had planned to think about on my retreat, but his words kept breaking in. "Why don't you give me your boredom?"

"No, I can't. Not that! I'll have to ask my wife. Can't I give you something else? You don't understand my situation. I won't."

For forty days I resisted.

On the fortieth day I rose up, left the monastery, and dumped my boredom into his lap. Do you know what he said?

XII

he Real Thing?

Christmas at the Monastery

For Christmas why don't you go to the Magic Monastery?

They have a Brother there who was one of the shepherds who first greeted the Christ Child. Of course this Brother is very old now, but when you hear him play his flute, you will become very young. (Be careful. You may do something silly.)

The three Wise Men are there also. Each Christmas one of them will give the sermon. Listen very carefully. You may have difficulty with his language, but that is because he is so wise and you are so foolish. I thought he was superficial, talking about incense on Christmas. It was only later that I realized he had been talking about the REAL incense, and now I can smell that wherever I go. Perhaps when you go there he will be speaking about the real gold, or the real myrrh.

And then there are the angels. You'll hear them singing. What shall I say? It's God's music. It gets into your bones. Nothing is the same afterwards.

But all this is nothing. What really matters is when the Word becomes flesh. Wait till you experience that.

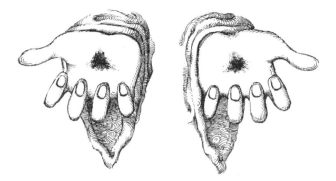

A Brother of St. Francis

When I told the guestmaster I was a Brother of St. Francis, he promptly asked me to come and tell the community about St. Francis. When I agreed, he seemed very pleased and went right out to ring the great bell. They came in by the hundreds, monks and nuns, and sat down on the floor. As soon as the guestmaster announced that I was a Brother of St. Francis, a buzz of excitement swept the room. In fact, so obvious was their delight, that I asked them how they had come to be so interested in St. Francis. A sprightly old nun stood up and said. "Why, he was here, didn't you know?" With the broadest of smiles she continued, "We invited him once to make our visitation." I was sure she was pulling my leg. "That man he did us so much good."

Then they began to tell me the beautiful things he said—and the funny things. They laughed and laughed. Then someone got up to show me how he danced. Soon they were all up, singing and dancing. All became quiet when an old monk started to tell how Brother Francis had spoken to them of the Passion of Christ, holding up his hand for all to see the wound. We wept, all of us. After a while I became aware that they had stopped, but I, I could not stop weeping. Then one by one they came, embraced me, and whispered, "Peace, Brother." Every last one of them came.

Seven Hundred Leagues

"Seven hundred leagues—it wasn't easy."

"But why didn't you go to join a monastery near you?"

"Because I had heard that this was a REAL monastery."